Thematic Units...

from The MAILBOX® magazine

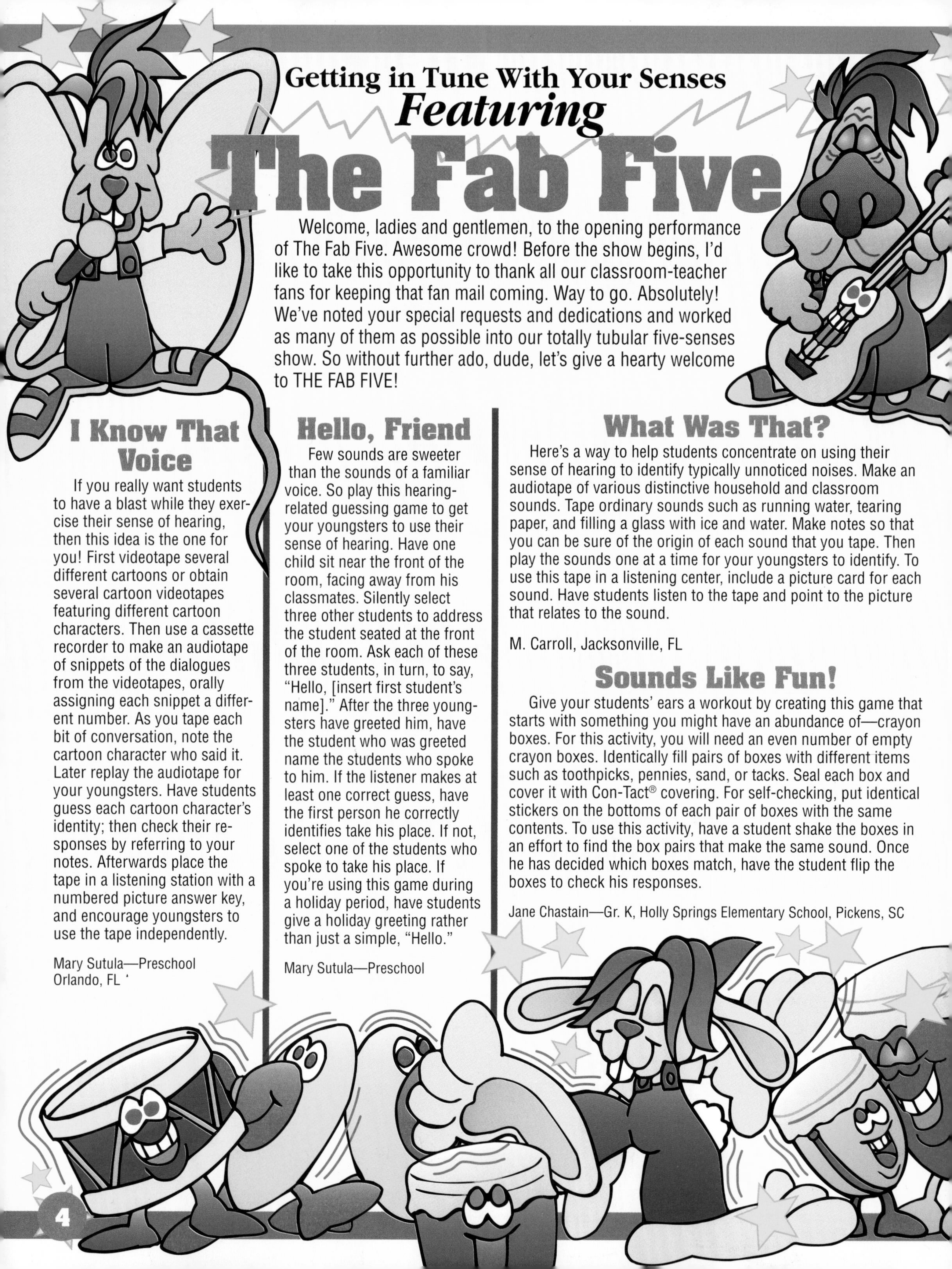

Getting in Tune With Your Senses

Featuring

The Fab Five

Welcome, ladies and gentlemen, to the opening performance of The Fab Five. Awesome crowd! Before the show begins, I'd like to take this opportunity to thank all our classroom-teacher fans for keeping that fan mail coming. Way to go. Absolutely! We've noted your special requests and dedications and worked as many of them as possible into our totally tubular five-senses show. So without further ado, dude, let's give a hearty welcome to THE FAB FIVE!

I Know That Voice

If you really want students to have a blast while they exercise their sense of hearing, then this idea is the one for you! First videotape several different cartoons or obtain several cartoon videotapes featuring different cartoon characters. Then use a cassette recorder to make an audiotape of snippets of the dialogues from the videotapes, orally assigning each snippet a different number. As you tape each bit of conversation, note the cartoon character who said it. Later replay the audiotape for your youngsters. Have students guess each cartoon character's identity; then check their responses by referring to your notes. Afterwards place the tape in a listening station with a numbered picture answer key, and encourage youngsters to use the tape independently.

Mary Sutula—Preschool
Orlando, FL

Hello, Friend

Few sounds are sweeter than the sounds of a familiar voice. So play this hearing-related guessing game to get your youngsters to use their sense of hearing. Have one child sit near the front of the room, facing away from his classmates. Silently select three other students to address the student seated at the front of the room. Ask each of these three students, in turn, to say, "Hello, [insert first student's name]." After the three youngsters have greeted him, have the student who was greeted name the students who spoke to him. If the listener makes at least one correct guess, have the first person he correctly identifies take his place. If not, select one of the students who spoke to take his place. If you're using this game during a holiday period, have students give a holiday greeting rather than just a simple, "Hello."

Mary Sutula—Preschool

What Was That?

Here's a way to help students concentrate on using their sense of hearing to identify typically unnoticed noises. Make an audiotape of various distinctive household and classroom sounds. Tape ordinary sounds such as running water, tearing paper, and filling a glass with ice and water. Make notes so that you can be sure of the origin of each sound that you tape. Then play the sounds one at a time for your youngsters to identify. To use this tape in a listening center, include a picture card for each sound. Have students listen to the tape and point to the picture that relates to the sound.

M. Carroll, Jacksonville, FL

Sounds Like Fun!

Give your students' ears a workout by creating this game that starts with something you might have an abundance of—crayon boxes. For this activity, you will need an even number of empty crayon boxes. Identically fill pairs of boxes with different items such as toothpicks, pennies, sand, or tacks. Seal each box and cover it with Con-Tact® covering. For self-checking, put identical stickers on the bottoms of each pair of boxes with the same contents. To use this activity, have a student shake the boxes in an effort to find the box pairs that make the same sound. Once he has decided which boxes match, have the student flip the boxes to check his responses.

Jane Chastain—Gr. K, Holly Springs Elementary School, Pickens, SC

The Five Senses

Preschool/Kindergarten

Table of Contents

Thematic Units

More Activities and Ideas

Reproducible Activities

Save time and energy planning thematic units with this comprehensive resource. We've searched the 1989–2001 issues of *The Mailbox*® and *Teacher's Helper*® magazines to find the best ideas for you to use when teaching a thematic unit about the five senses. Included in this book are favorite units from the magazines, single ideas to extend a unit, and a variety of reproducible activities. Pick and choose from these activities to develop your own complete unit or simply to enhance your current lesson plans. You're sure to find everything you need for active learning fun.

Project Managers: Sherri Lynn Kuntz, Scott Lyons
Copy Editors: Sylvan Allen, Gina Farago, Karen Brewer Grossman, Karen L. Huffman, Amy Kirtley-Hill, Debbie Shoffner
Cover Artists: Nick Greenwood, Kimberly Richard
Artist: Rebecca Saunders
Typesetters: Lynette Dickerson, Mark Rainey

www.themailbox.com

ISBN10 #1-56234-487-0 • ISBN13 #978-1-56234-487-0

Printed in the United States
10 9 8 7

RRDRO041142657

"Touch Me" Book

Youngsters won't want to take their hands off these books. Begin this project by asking each youngster to contribute 2" x 4" rectangles of various textured materials to be made into a book. Provide additional textured samples. Once your collection of textures is complete, have each youngster incorporate several into a booklet. Encourage each child to share his booklet with others and describe each of the textures it contains.

Doris Russell, Sun Prairie, WI

Textures Around Us

Challenge your little ones to investigate the textures in the natural world around them. Divide your students into small groups, and have them walk around your school. Encourage students to find something that looks as though it would have an interesting texture or feel. Before permitting them to touch the selected item, photograph the group members with the item and ask them to predict how it will feel. Then encourage each group member to touch and describe the texture of the object. Note each group's description. Find out whether or not students' predictions were accurate. When the pictures have been developed, glue each one into a blank booklet and write the youngsters' descriptions beneath the picture.

Sheli Gossett—Gr. K, Sebring, FL

Screening

With this idea, the sense of touch is the focal point both during the process and, inherently, in the result. In preparation for this activity, staple a piece of screen to an identically sized piece of cardboard. Then use wide tape to tape the screen securely to the cardboard. Provide a supply of crayons and paper for students to use with the screen. Encourage each youngster to bear down a little more than normal as he takes a turn writing or drawing on a sheet of paper placed on top of the screen. Once the child has done this, have him feel the texture of his work and comment on how it feels to the touch.

Ariela L. Mahoney—Gr. K
Mitchell School
Needham, MA

It's in the Bag

Using his sense of touch, each youngster can match an unseen item to the picture card that corresponds to it. Make a few small cloth bags or use old socks for this purpose. Collect some small household items that will fit into the bags or socks you will use. Make a picture card to represent each item; then place each item in a bag (or sock) and stitch (or tie) the opening. Place the cards and the bags in a center. Have students take turns feeling the objects inside the bags and matching each bag to a picture.

Jane Chastain—Gr. K
Holly Springs Elementary School
Pickens, SC

Variation on Turtle Shells

It won't take much enticement to get your youngsters to rub the backs of these student-made textured turtles. To make a turtle shell, paint the back of a six-inch paper plate green. Cut a turtle head, legs, and tail from construction paper and glue them to the unpainted side of the plate. Add details with a marker if desired. Choose four fabrics or other materials that have interesting textures (such as corduroy, fake fur, sandpaper, and satin). Cut them into triangular swatches, and glue them to the painted side of the plate to complete the turtle.

Joy Bressler—Gr. K
Fort Miami Elementary School
Maumee, OH

Get the Picture?

The sense of sight is the focus of this engaging activity. Cut out pictures from magazines and glue each of them to a sheet of paper. Or draw and color several different pictures, each on a different sheet of paper. Place an identically sized sheet of construction paper on top of each sheet of paper. Tape the tops of the paired pages together. Draw lines to visually divide the construction paper vertically into thirds, and cut only through the construction paper along the lines. (If the picture is symmetrical, divide and cut the construction paper in half.) To use each of these pictures, a student starts with the construction-paper flaps down. Lifting the flap to the left, he tries to identify the partially hidden picture. If that's not enough information, he lifts the next flap on the left. Finally he lifts the last flap to reveal the picture or to confirm his guess.

Virginia Chaverri—Gr. Pre/K

Scented Rainbow

Tease the eyes—as well as the nose—with these beautiful rainbow-shape booklets. Provide each child with six arch-shaped booklet pages containing the following programming: "[Fill in word to describe the smell] as a [fill in name of fruit illustrated]." Show students the flavored gelatin they'll be using to decorate their pages. For instance, you might supply powdered gelatin in the following flavors: cherry (red), orange (orange), lemon (yellow), lime (green), blueberry (blue), and grape (purple). Given these gelatins, have the students draw cherries on the first page and color some of them. To "colorize" the others, have each student put glue on the cherry design, then sprinkle on cherry-flavored gelatin. Encourage each youngster to sniff the fragrance given off by the gelatin and dictate a word that describes the smell. Write (or have the youngster write) to fill in the blanks on the page. When each of the remaining five pages has been completed in the same way (which may be done over the course of several days), have each student staple his dried pages beneath an arch-shaped cover. To extend the olfactory theme, have students "colorize" their rainbow covers using scented markers to make bands of color.

Sheli Gossett, Sebring, FL

Sensory Strolls

Youngsters can walk their way to sensory awareness. Begin by taking your students on a walk around school. Ask them to name all the different things that they see. Take another walk on another day, but this time have students name everything they can hear. On subsequent days, have students take other walks specifically to explore their senses of touch and smell. To explore students' sense of taste, pack some bite-size treats that are sweet (fruit candy), sour (pickles), salty (pretzels), and bitter (bittersweet chocolate), and take them along on a walk. Pause to picnic on the treats and discuss the differences in the tastes.

Cara Schlotter—Preschool, Faith Christian Child Care, Washington, IL

Interactive Display

Near the conclusion of your unit on the five senses, get students involved in creating collages and interactive displays that represent the senses. Have students work in small groups to create five collages, each of which features one of these body parts: eyes, ears, noses, hands, or mouths. Display each of the collages, and set up a companion display nearby that is indicative of the sense being depicted. For example, in front of the eyes collage could be a display containing glasses, goggles, a microscope, binoculars, mirrors, and magnifying glasses. Musical instruments, different sizes of bells, books with musical or sound effects, a cassette player, and a recording of environmental sounds could be arranged in front of the ears collage. And cotton balls scented with peppermint, cloves, cinnamon, vinegar, and onions could be placed in front of the nose collage, along with fragrant flowers and perfumes. Add interest in front of the hands collage by accompanying it with a "feely box" and a banner with lots of different textures on it. Top off the mouth collage with food items such as lemon balls, pretzels, pickles, bittersweet chocolate, and something sweet. Then invite everyone to explore and enjoy.

Sandra Ziegler—Preschool, St. Mary's Catholic School, Strongsville, OH

Christine Wirtanen, Northeast, Evergreen Park, IL

Singing the Senses

Here's a song that will leave you with an earful—of a sensory song, that is.

(sung to the tune of "Bingo")

We use five senses every day
To help us learn and play.
See, hear, smell, touch, taste.
See, hear, smell, touch, taste.
See, hear, smell, touch, taste.
We do these every day.

Penni Flood—Pre/K
Park Village Elementary
San Antonio, TX

Bread-Making Bonanza

Baking bread can be a sensory bonanza for your class. Prepare two loaves of dough for the oven before class, and begin baking them just before you and your students begin mixing the ingredients for another two loaves. Let the second batch of dough rise; then gather the children around to punch it down and take turns kneading it. While baking bread, youngsters can see how flour and yeast turn into a brown crusty loaf. They can feel the texture of the dough and the bread. They can smell the aroma of the baking bread and taste the flavor once it's done. And what will they hear? "Mmmmmm!"

Doris Russell, Sun Prairie, WI

Water Play

Mix children, water, rocks, and scrub brushes. What have you got? You've got one great sensory experience! Place several large rocks of various textures and colors in the water table. Also include several sizes and types of scrub brushes and food coloring or liquid dish soap. Ask youngsters to scrub the rocks clean. The brushes will make interesting sounds; the rocks, dish soap, and food coloring will create interesting visual images; and the rocks, soap, and water all have fascinating textures to feel.

Susan Anker—Pre/K
Early Childhood Family Education Center
White Bear Lake, MN

A Trip Down Sensory Lane

Why not end your five-senses unit with a thematic flair? Using the descriptions below, set up a variety of specialty shops straight out of the early 1900s. Students will delight in visiting the unusual shops and testing out their senses. The end result—a culminating activity with sensory appeal!

- **Optical Review:** At this Wild West show, feature a clip from a 3-D movie or a collection of optical illusions.
- **Doctor Twin, M.D.:** For this shop enlist an eye-care professional to share information about eyes and proper eye care. An assortment of visual discrimination games could also be featured.
- **The Vibration Station:** Display an assortment of vibrating instruments such as tuning forks, guitars, and drums at this station. Students can stop by and fine-tune their hearing.
- **Firehouse Antics:** Students are all ears at the firehouse! Without revealing her sources, the Fire Chief (an adult volunteer) creates different sounds by tapping together and/or dropping a variety of unbreakable objects. Students try to identify how each sound is made.
- **The Perfumery:** Fill this shop with a collection of sniffing canisters and cutouts. To make a sniffing canister, dab a cotton ball with a desired scent and tuck the cotton ball inside an empty, plastic film canister. Punch a small hole in the canister's lid before snapping it in place. Then create a cutout that reveals the source of each smell (for example, a strawberry cutout for a strawberry scent and a vanilla bean cutout for a vanilla scent). Students sniff the canisters and match them to the appropriate cutouts.
- **The Sniff Smith:** At this shop, students find out how the sense of smell affects their sense of taste. Provide a sampling of unidentifiable foods. Students pinch their noses as they sample each food and try to determine its flavor. (To make foods unidentifiable, blend them in a food processor.)
- **The Tastery:** At this place of business, students use their taste buds to identify visually indistinguishable foods. Salt, white sugar, baking soda, and flour can be tasted. Or peel and dice raw apples, pears, and potatoes for sampling.
- **The Candy Shop:** Sweet (sugar), sour (lemon or pickle juice), bitter (powdered cocoa), and salty (salt) are tasted at this eatery. If desired, display a diagram that shows where each type of taste bud is found on the tongue.
- **The Feel Mercantile:** At this general store, each product is inside a burlap bag. Students try to determine what products are for sale by feeling the bags.
- **Rub-a-Dub Bathhouse:** Place several small items—such as erasers, pom-poms, golf balls, and plastic combs—in the bottom of a plastic tub or pool before filling the container with packing pellets. Students try to identify the objects under the pellets by touch. To check their hunches, they pull the objects to the surface.

Jean Wark—Gr. K, Perkins Elementary, St. Petersburg, FL

Senses All Around

Wrap up your study of the five senses with a sensory fair. Make plans to feature one or more center activities for each sense. (See the list of suggestions below.) In a parent note, explain the event and request needed supplies. Also enlist the help of several adult volunteers—at least one per center. To stage the event, arrange the adult-supervised center activities around the classroom. Then, under your direction, have students move from center to center along a predetermined route. Let's go to the fair!

Center suggestions:

- **Touch:** For this center, prepare one or more "feely boxes." To make a "feely box," remove the lid and cut an opening from each end of a shoebox. (A youngster must be able to slide one hand into each opening.) Fill the box with pairs of small items; then replace the box lid. A student slides his hands through the openings and feels the contents of the box. When the student thinks he's found two identical objects, he asks a parent volunteer or a classmate to remove the box lid so that he can check his work.
- **Hearing:** To make this center, you will need a supply of duplicated sound cards like the ones shown. A student arranges several cards in a row; then he performs the sounds in order by following the visual clues on his cards.
- **Sight:** Place a variety of optical devices—such as magnifying lenses, sunglasses, binoculars, and hand mirrors—at this exploration center. Once students have explored the optical apparatuses, the adult volunteer can engage students in a memory game in which the players try to determine which object the adult has removed from the collection.
- **Taste:** Slice or dice a variety of exotic fruits like mangoes, kiwi-fruits, papayas, passion fruits, and pineapple for this center. Display the fruit pieces and a supply of toothpicks. A student uses a toothpick to poke and sample a variety of fruits.
- **Smell:** For this center, place a different flavor of gelatin powder and/or ground spice in each of several small containers. A student sniffs the contents of each container in an effort to identify the corresponding smell. When all of the containers have been sniffed by a child or a group of children, the parent volunteer reveals the source of each smell. Next, on a sheet of drawing paper, each student illustrates one fruit or spice he smelled at the center. The parent volunteer uses double-sided tape to attach a sample of the corresponding powder to the student's completed project.

Doris Russell, Sun Prairie, WI

A Poppin' Good Time

Pop! Sniff! Crunch! Here's the perfect ending to a "sense-ational" unit! Under the watchful eyes of your youngsters, pop a sizable amount of popcorn kernels using an air popper. As the corn is popping, ask students to describe the sights, sounds, and smells of the popping corn. Also place a small container of popped and unpopped kernels at each table, and ask students to feel and describe the differences between the two forms of corn. Finally give each youngster a serving of popped corn and have him put his taste buds to the test. If desired, serve students small samplings of differently seasoned popcorn (such as salted, buttered, salted and buttered) and ask students to identify the different tastes; then record your youngsters' popcorn preferences on a class graph. Now that's wrapping up a unit in good taste!

Tina Nowakowski—Gr. K
East End Elementary
Humboldt, TN

What a Sight!

Take an insightful look at our sense of sight with Ed Young's delightful book *Seven Blind Mice* (published by Philomel Books). As the story unfolds, each of six colorful mice sizes up an unidentified object with different results. It's not until the seventh mouse sizes up the whole object that its true identity is revealed. To prepare a fun lead-in activity to the story, cut several pictures of large objects from discarded magazines. Snip each object in half. Display one part of each picture on the chalkboard and set aside the remaining cutouts for later use. To begin the activity, ask students to study the partial pictures on display and suggest what each object could be. List the students' predictions below the appropriate pictures. Take a moment to discuss what makes this activity challenging; then read aloud the insightful mice tale. At the conclusion of the story, use the cutouts that were previously set aside to piece together the pictures on display. Much like the mice in the story, students are sure to conclude that our sense of sight is most valuable when we take the time to view things in their entirety.

Kathy Curnow—Gr. K
Woolridge Elementary
Midlothian, VA

The "Sense-sational" Sensory Fair

Come one, come all to the Sensory Fair! Invite youngsters and their parents to explore and review the senses with these hands-on activities. Your classroom will be a place for fun and discovery with a classroom Sensory Fair.

by Marie Iannetti

Setting Up and Getting Ready

Send a completed copy of the parent note (page 14) home with each child. To prepare your classroom for the Sensory Fair, decorate with items such as balloons, crepe paper, and banners. To the front door of the room, tape a sign that reads "The Sensory Fair." Set up an area in your room for each activity in this unit. Display a sign near each center identifying the sense or senses used in that activity. Mount step-by-step directions at each area. Discuss the directions with your class. On the day of the fair, have students escort their parents as they visit each area.

Sight

Seeing is believing with this activity. Place a supply of small blocks and blindfolds in a center. Have students and parents visiting this center alternate wearing the blindfolds. Using the blocks, have each person attempt to build a tower. Then have them remove their blindfolds and build a tower with the use of their eyesight. Have them discuss the differences in both versions.

Your little ones will be wide-eyed when they examine the real importance of the sense of sight. Cut several eyeglass-frame shapes from double thicknesses of construction paper. Glue waxed paper between each pair of construction-paper frames so that the waxed paper covers each of the lens areas. Have each child and parent visiting the center alternate wearing a pair of these glasses while attempting to do a task such as putting a puzzle together or tying a shoelace. Then have him remove his glasses and discuss the activity with the other member of his group.

Hearing

Before parents and students visit this area, have a volunteer hide several familiar rhythm instruments behind a draped table. Have the volunteer play one instrument at a time, without displaying it. Encourage parents and students to use their sense of hearing to identify each instrument.

Naming that sound will be the object of this "sound-sational" idea. Place a tape player in a corner of your room with a tape of recorded sounds such as a door slamming, a bell ringing, water trickling, a vacuum cleaner sweeping, a telephone ringing, or a balloon bursting. Display an answer sheet nearby for parents' use. To use this center, encourage students and parents to use their sense of hearing to identify each sound.

Taste

Set up a tasting table in your room. Fill each of several paper plates with a different type of food such as salted popcorn, salted crackers, unsweetened chocolate, lemon slices, sour pickles, cookies, and marshmallows. Provide a duplicated supply of the reproducible on page 15. Have the visitors in the center taste each food and describe how it tastes. Then instruct them to draw a picture of each of the foods in the corresponding box.

It's the battle of the soft drinks! Challenge your little ones and their caregivers to use their sense of taste to tell them apart. Label the bottoms of some paper cups with "cola" and some with "diet cola." Fill each cup halfway with the corresponding cola. Have the participants at this center take a sip of the cola, then a sip of the diet cola. Ask if they can tell which is which.

Touch

This center is a touch-and-match activity. Fill brown paper bags with several pairs of objects such as paper clips, dice, marbles, crayons, buttons, and milk-jug lids. Place the bags on a table at a center. To use this center—without looking in the bags— the participants touch the objects in the bags. Using their sense of touch, they try to find matching objects. When they think they have found a match, they take the objects out to check. Placing each pair of objects on the table, they continue in this manner until all of the matching pairs have been identified.

Touch and tell is the name of the game at this center. Cut a hole—large enough for a hand to fit through—in the bottom of a box. Then gather a supply of items with interesting textures such as a banana, an orange, uncooked pasta, cooked spaghetti, a walnut, and a chilled canned soft drink. Place these items in an opaque bag. To do this activity, have the parent stand the box on end with the open end facing away from the child. Next have the parent (secretly) place one of the items in the box. Then instruct the child to insert his hand through the hole and feel the object. Encourage him to use his sense of touch to identify the object. Have the parent and child continue in this manner until all of the objects have been guessed.

Smell

In advance, collect a variety of scented items such as coffee grains, perfume, onion, lemon, soap, peanut butter, and cinnamon. Wrap a small portion of each item or a sample on a cotton ball in a piece of gauze, and place it in an opaque container with a lid. Label the bottom of each container with its contents. Place the containers in a center. To use this center, have an adult lift the lid from a container and hold the container under the child's nose. Have the child smell the contents of each container and guess what it is.

Have the participants in this center make a scented picture. Stock a center with dark-colored construction paper and a variety of different scented soaps. To use the center, the participants use the soap to draw the design of their choice on the construction paper. Mmm...can you smell it?

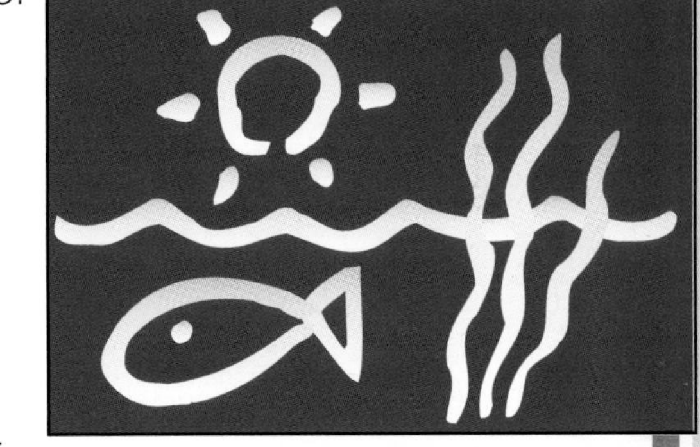

Invite parents and children to make a scented potpourri sachet at this center. Stock a center with a large bag of potpourri, net, rulers, scissors, gold wired ribbon, and rubber bands. To make a sachet, have parents assist each student in cutting a 14-inch circle of net. Have each child place a portion of potpourri in the center of the net. Have him gather the net around the potpourri and secure the top with a rubber band. Tie a length of gold wired ribbon around the rubber band; then tie a bow.

Parent Note

Use with "Setting Up and Getting Ready" on page 10.

Dear Parent,

Our class has been learning about the five senses. You are invited to a Sensory Fair on

_________________________ at _________________________.
(date) (time)

We'd like you to participate with us in some fun sensory activities and see what we have learned!

Hope to see you there!

____
(teacher)

Dear Parent,

Our class has been learning about the five senses. You are invited to a Sensory Fair on

_________________________ at _________________________.
(date) (time)

We'd like you to participate with us in some fun sensory activities and see what we have learned!

Hope to see you there!

____
(teacher)

©The Education Center, Inc. • *Five Senses* • Preschool/Kindergarten • TEC3233

Name ______________________________

Note to the teacher: Use with the first tasting activity on page 11.

A GINGERBREAD "SENSE-SATION"

These activities add a touch of gingerbread and a flavor of fun to stir up some five-senses learning experiences for your youngsters.

ideas contributed by Kathy Curnow

AN INVITATION TEMPTATION

Stimulate the curiosity and senses of your little ones with this eye-appealing, sense-tickling door display. To make it, tape a length of brown bulletin-board paper along your classroom door frame. Trim the paper above the door to resemble a roof. Edge the house with scalloped bulletin-board trim; then paint details on the house. Next give each child a construction-paper circle and have him glue a photo of himself to the center of it. Then encourage him to decorate his cutout in lollipop-style. To add fragrance to his lollipop, have him squeeze a line of glue along the edge of his circle, then sprinkle on ground cinnamon, cloves, or a flavored gelatin mix. After the glue dries, tape the end of a wide craft stick to the cutout. Attach the completed lollipops to the gingerbread-house display to make an inviting grand entry into the "scent-sational" world of gingerbread.

GINGERBREAD LISTENING

Highlight each child's sense of hearing by presenting a hearing-oriented storytime. Read aloud Paul Galdone's *The Gingerbread Boy* (Clarion Books), but do not show the pictures. Encourage each child to close his eyes and use his sense of hearing to imagine what is happening in the story. Afterward, ask children questions about the story. As youngsters respond to your questions, ask how they knew the answers—since they couldn't even see the pictures! Guide youngsters to conclude that they could follow the story because they used their sense of hearing.

YOO-HOO! WHERE ARE YOU?

After reading the story without pictures (see "Gingerbread Listening"), invite students to participate in this game requiring sharp listening skills. In advance, duplicate one gingerbread-boy pattern (page 18) on construction paper. Cut out the pattern; then decorate it as desired. Attach a craft stick to create a stick puppet. Seat students in a circle. Designate one child to be It and to sit in the middle of the circle with her eyes closed. Then play some music and have the other students pass the puppet from child to child. Stop the music and have the child with the puppet hold it. Then instruct It, with her eyes closed, to say, "Yoo-hoo! Where are you?" Ask the child with the puppet to respond, "Here I am!" It uses her sense of hearing to identify who has the gingerbread boy. After the child is identified, she exchanges places with It. Continue in the same manner, giving each child an opportunity to be It.

GINGERBREAD VIEWERS

And now for the sense of sight! Review *The Gingerbread Boy* (see "Gingerbread Listening") with your students. Ask questions that students might only know for sure by using their sense of sight. (For example, you might ask, "What color are the Gingerbread Boy's shoes?") When you begin to get varying answers or questions, invite your youngsters to use their sense of sight as you reread the story and show the illustrations. Then ask the same questions that you asked at the beginning of this activity. Emphasize how each child's sense of sight provided him with more information.

TOUCH AND TELL

Youngsters may be quite interested to learn that hearing and seeing are not the only senses that provide us with information—the sense of touch can provide lots of information, too. Invite students to play a tactile matching game. Use the pattern on page 18 to make several pairs of tagboard gingerbread boys. Apply a different texture to each pair of cutouts. For example, to one pair, glue on sandpaper. To another pair, glue on stretched-out cotton balls. To a third pair, use craft glue to glue on aquarium gravel. To a fourth pair, glue on identical fabrics. When each set is dry, invite students to play a touch-and-tell matching game. To play, have a child close his eyes; then give him a gingerbread boy. Place its match and an additional gingerbread boy in front of the child. Encourage him to carefully feel the gingerbread boy he is holding, then feel the others to find its match. After he identifies the matching gingerbread boy, have him open his eyes and use his sense of sight to check his choice. A lot can be learned through touch alone!

THE NOSE KNOWS

Out of sight? Out of earshot? Out of touch? Then stimulate those sniffers and try smelling it out! In advance, prepare two different flavors of Jell-O® Jigglers® according to the package directions. Also follow the provided recipe to prepare a stiff batch of cinnamon-flavored gelatin. After each flavor of gelatin has set, cut out small gingerbread-boy shapes using cookie cutters. Put a spoonful of cinnamon in a paper cup. Then place a gelatin gingerbread boy of each flavor on separate paper plates. Cover each plate with a paper towel. First have a volunteer smell the cinnamon in the cup; then ask him to smell the gelatin on each plate (without looking) to determine which one matches the aroma of the cinnamon. When he discovers the match, ask him to use his sense of sight to check his selection. Afterward, invite him to eat one of the Jigglers®. Then replace the selected gelatin with one of the same flavor and repeat the exercise, giving each child an opportunity to sniff and match.

Cinnamon Gelatin

2 envelopes unflavored gelatin
1/2 tbs. cinnamon
3 tbs. sugar
1/2 cup cold water
1 1/2 cups boiling water

In a large bowl, sprinkle the cold water over the gelatin. Let the mix stand for one minute; then stir in the cinnamon and sugar. Add the boiling water and stir the ingredients together until the gelatin and sugar dissolve (the cinnamon will remain grainy). Chill the gelatin until firm.

ACTIVATE ALL SENSES

With all these gingerbread activities, your youngsters will be primed for a total sensory experience resulting in a treat they can sink their teeth into—gingerbread cookies! In advance, make a chart with a column labeled for each of the five senses. With the help of students, prepare gingerbread cookies following the provided recipe. As you do, ask children to comment on the many things they see, hear, feel, smell, and taste. Record youngsters' comments on the chart. Students are sure to be motivated when their senses are activated.

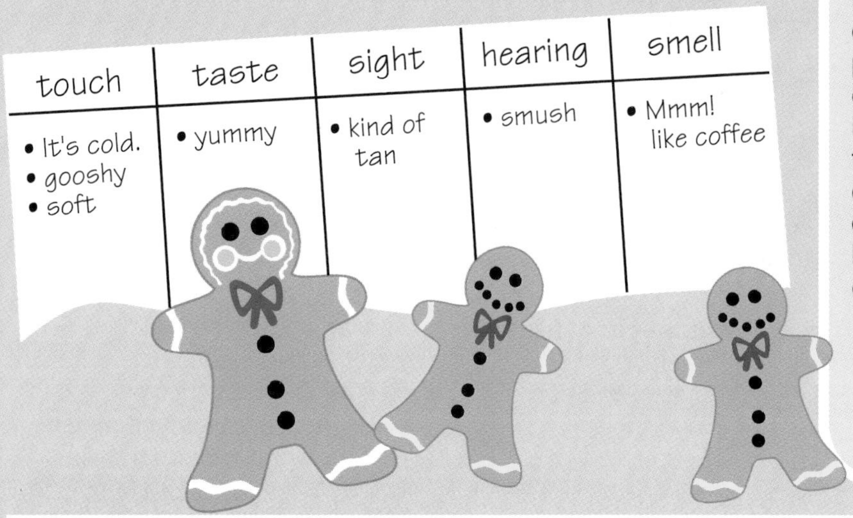

touch	taste	sight	hearing	smell
• It's cold. • gooshy • soft	• yummy	• kind of tan	• smush	• Mmm! like coffee

GINGERBREAD COOKIES

(makes approximately 30 cookies)

1 cup sugar
3/4 cup shortening
1 egg
1/4 cup molasses
2 cups plain flour, sifted
2 tsp. baking soda
1/4 tsp. salt
1 tsp. cinnamon
3/4 tsp. cloves
3/4 tsp. ginger

Preheat the oven to 375°F. Combine and mix the first four ingredients in a large bowl. Add the remaining ingredients and mix well to form a dough. Roll the dough onto a sheet of waxed paper. Cut the dough with gingerbread-man cookie cutters; then place the cookies two inches apart on a greased cookie sheet. Bake the cookies 10–12 minutes. After the cookies cool, have each child use tube icing to decorate a cookie as desired. Then invite him to enjoy the sweet sensation of eating his cookie.

Gingerbread-Boy Pattern

Use with "Yoo-Hoo! Where Are You?" on page 16 and "Touch and Tell" on page 17.

Discover the Five Senses

Preschoolers are natural explorers. When they explore, they discover. And when they discover, they *learn!* In this unit you'll find suggestions for setting up exploration centers that help children discover one of the five senses each week. You'll also find weekly notes that get families involved in the discoveries!

ideas by Katy Zoldak—Pre-K, Special Education, Metzenbaum School, Parma, OH

ROAR

Hearing

Exploration Center

Hear, hear! Try adding these items to your center to help youngsters explore sound.

- tape recorder with headphones and cassette tapes
- musical instruments
- microphone with amplifier (Consider designating times when this can be used.)
- small, sealed boxes that you have filled with different items, such as beans, jingle bells, etc.
- tube telephone (To make one, use electrical tape to secure a plastic funnel to each end of a 15-foot-long plastic tube. The plastic tubes are available at home-supply stores.)

Family Activity

Prepare this family activity several weeks before beginning your study of the senses. Put a blank cassette tape in a battery-operated tape recorder. Put the recorder and a copy of the note below in a tote bag. Send the bag home with a different child each night. When every child has had an opportunity to record household sounds, play the tape during a group time. Make a list of all of the sounds that your class identifies. Then place the tape in your exploration center.

Dear Caregiver,

We're discovering the sense of sound! Would you please help us in our explorations? In this bag, you'll find a tape recorder with a tape in it. Please record your child's name; then help him/her record five household sounds, such as a baby crying or the television. (You do not need to rewind the tape before or after recording your sounds.) Return the bag to school tomorrow.

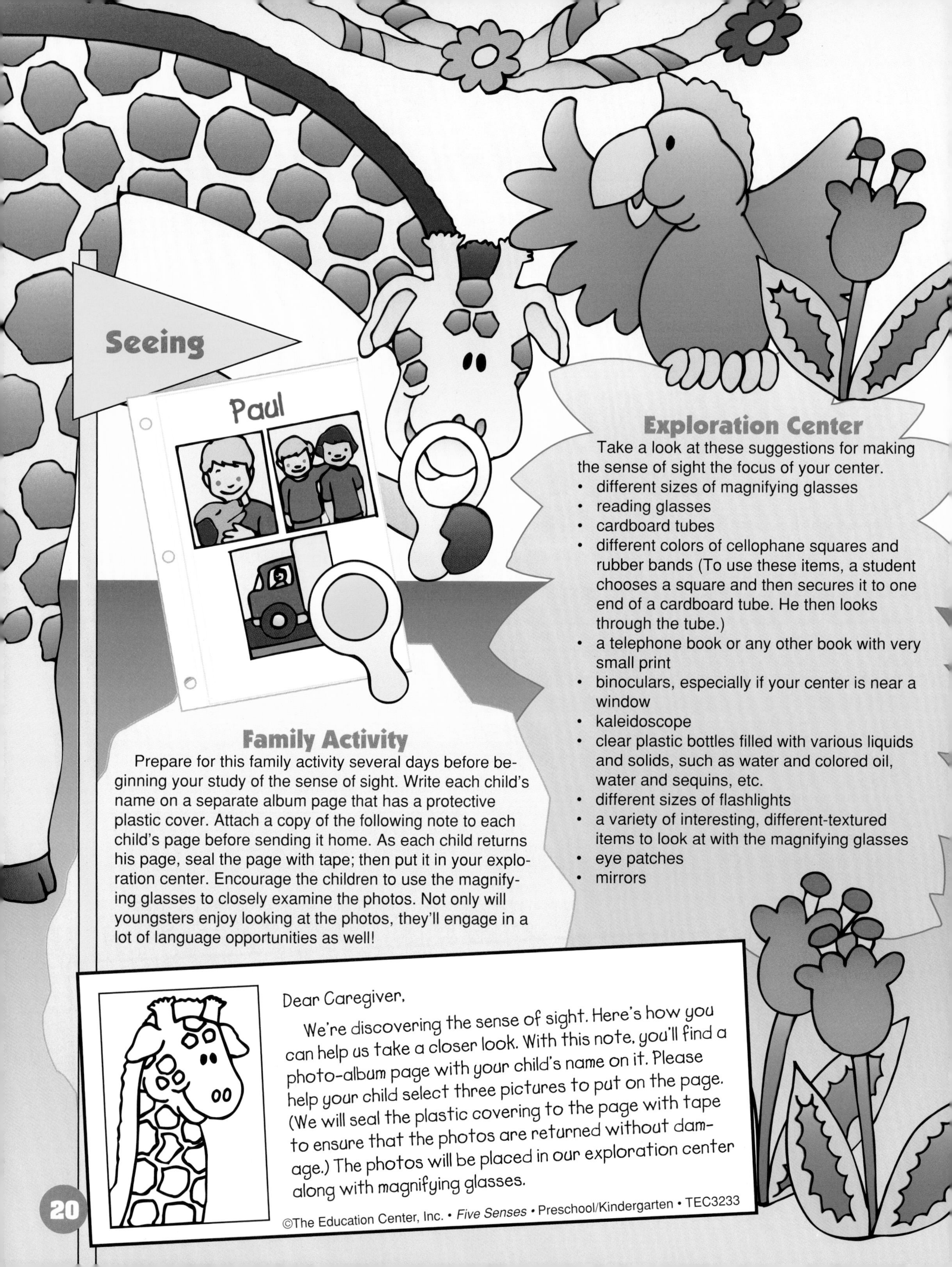

Exploration Center

Take a look at these suggestions for making the sense of sight the focus of your center.

- different sizes of magnifying glasses
- reading glasses
- cardboard tubes
- different colors of cellophane squares and rubber bands (To use these items, a student chooses a square and then secures it to one end of a cardboard tube. He then looks through the tube.)
- a telephone book or any other book with very small print
- binoculars, especially if your center is near a window
- kaleidoscope
- clear plastic bottles filled with various liquids and solids, such as water and colored oil, water and sequins, etc.
- different sizes of flashlights
- a variety of interesting, different-textured items to look at with the magnifying glasses
- eye patches
- mirrors

Family Activity

Prepare for this family activity several days before beginning your study of the sense of sight. Write each child's name on a separate album page that has a protective plastic cover. Attach a copy of the following note to each child's page before sending it home. As each child returns his page, seal the page with tape; then put it in your exploration center. Encourage the children to use the magnifying glasses to closely examine the photos. Not only will youngsters enjoy looking at the photos, they'll engage in a lot of language opportunities as well!

Dear Caregiver,

We're discovering the sense of sight. Here's how you can help us take a closer look. With this note, you'll find a photo-album page with your child's name on it. Please help your child select three pictures to put on the page. (We will seal the plastic covering to the page with tape to ensure that the photos are returned without damage.) The photos will be placed in our exploration center along with magnifying glasses.

Exploration Center

Youngsters are sure to get a feel for the sense of touch when you add these items to your exploration center. (To avoid tactile messes, you may want to carefully consider the combination of items you put in the center at one time.)

- play dough
- ice packs and gel-filled ice packs
- plastic ice cubes in novelty shapes and colors
- zippered plastic bags filled with various liquids, such as tempera paint, fingerpaint, shampoo, etc. (Seal the bags closed with clear packing tape.)
- hot water bottle
- blindfolds
- a variety of other different-textured objects and materials, such as sandpaper, sponges, etc.

Family Activity

Use this activity to ask parents to help you during your study of the sense of touch. Personalize a paper lunch bag for each child; then attach a copy of the note below. Send the bags home. The next day collect the bags and bring them to your group time. Select a bag. Ask each child to put his hand in the bag and feel the object. When everyone has felt the item, have the group guess what it is. Then reveal the object and thank the child who brought it to school. Continue until all of the items have been discovered.

Dear Caregiver,

We're exploring the sense of touch. Here's how you can help us get a real feel for the topic! Please help your child find an item that has an interesting texture (such as a sponge or cotton ball) to put in the attached paper bag. Return the bag to school tomorrow. During a group time, we are going to try to guess what the item is just by using our sense of touch. Please indicate if you would like for the item to be returned after our activity.

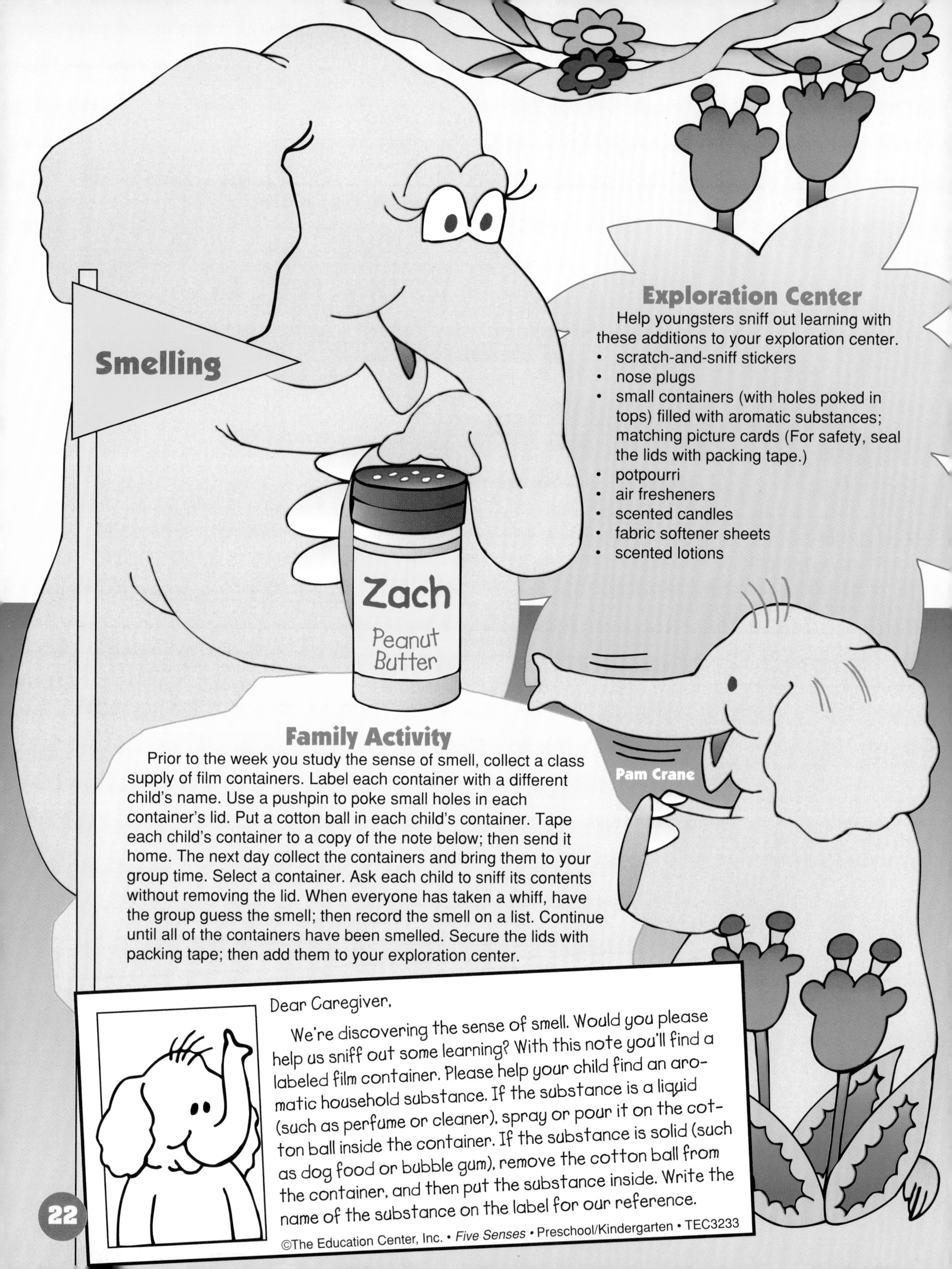

Smelling

Exploration Center

Help youngsters sniff out learning with these additions to your exploration center.

- scratch-and-sniff stickers
- nose plugs
- small containers (with holes poked in tops) filled with aromatic substances; matching picture cards (For safety, seal the lids with packing tape.)
- potpourri
- air fresheners
- scented candles
- fabric softener sheets
- scented lotions

Family Activity

Prior to the week you study the sense of smell, collect a class supply of film containers. Label each container with a different child's name. Use a pushpin to poke small holes in each container's lid. Put a cotton ball in each child's container. Tape each child's container to a copy of the note below; then send it home. The next day collect the containers and bring them to your group time. Select a container. Ask each child to sniff its contents without removing the lid. When everyone has taken a whiff, have the group guess the smell; then record the smell on a list. Continue until all of the containers have been smelled. Secure the lids with packing tape; then add them to your exploration center.

Dear Caregiver,

We're discovering the sense of smell. Would you please help us sniff out some learning? With this note you'll find a labeled film container. Please help your child find an aromatic household substance. If the substance is a liquid (such as perfume or cleaner), spray or pour it on the cotton ball inside the container. If the substance is solid (such as dog food or bubble gum), remove the cotton ball from the container, and then put the substance inside. Write the name of the substance on the label for our reference.

Tasting

Exploration Center

Each day that you study the sense of taste, set up a different tasting station at your exploration center using the ideas below. Provide napkins, cups, and a pitcher of water, if desired. Before students begin visiting the center, talk about good health habits, such as washing hands and not touching each other's food. Supervise the visits to the center more closely than in previous weeks.

- Provide individual portions of salty items in paper cups.
- Provide individual portions of sweet items in paper cups.
- Provide individual portions of fruit chunks in paper cups.
- Provide individual portions of vegetables in resealable plastic bags along with individual cups of dip.
- Provide a variety of sauces and spreads in bowls. Give each child a number of cracker pieces. Instruct him to dip each cracker piece once into a sauce or spread that he would like to try.

Family Activity

To prepare for a group taste-testing activity, write each child's name on a separate resealable plastic bag. Put a copy of the following note in each child's bag; then send the bags home. The next day collect the bags and bring them to your group time. Select one of the bags and give every child a taste. Record whether the food was sweet, salty, spicy, sour, or bitter by making a simple graph like the one shown. Continue until all of the items have been tasted.

sweet	salty	spicy	sour	bitter
sugar	pretzels			
chocolate chips	potato chips		lemon juice	

Dear Caregiver,

We are discovering the sense of taste. Please help us have a taste-testing party. Assist your child in finding a food or sauce to put in this plastic resealable bag. We only need a very small portion for each child to taste. For example, include a quarter of a pickle for each child or enough sauce and small cracker pieces for each child to take a dip. Write the name of the food on the bag; then return it to school tomorrow. During our group time, we will taste the food. Then we will chart whether the food is sweet, salty, spicy, sour, or bitter.

“Sense-sational”

Elephant “Feely Box”

Your little ones will have tons of guessing fun with this “feely-box” activity. Paint a medium-sized cardboard box gray. When the paint is dry, cut a hole that is big enough for a child’s hand to fit through in the center of one side of the box. Cut the arm from a discarded gray sweatshirt. Hot-glue the cut edge of the sleeve around the hole along the inside of the box to resemble an elephant’s trunk. Use a marker to draw eyes above the trunk. Cut out elephant-ear shapes from construction paper; then glue them to opposite sides of the box. Fill the box with an assortment of objects. To use the box, a child pushes his hand through the elephant’s trunk and attempts to identify an object in the box. He then pulls the object out and verifies his guesses.

Diane Friedlein—Preschool
Head Start—Manchester II
Manchester, IA

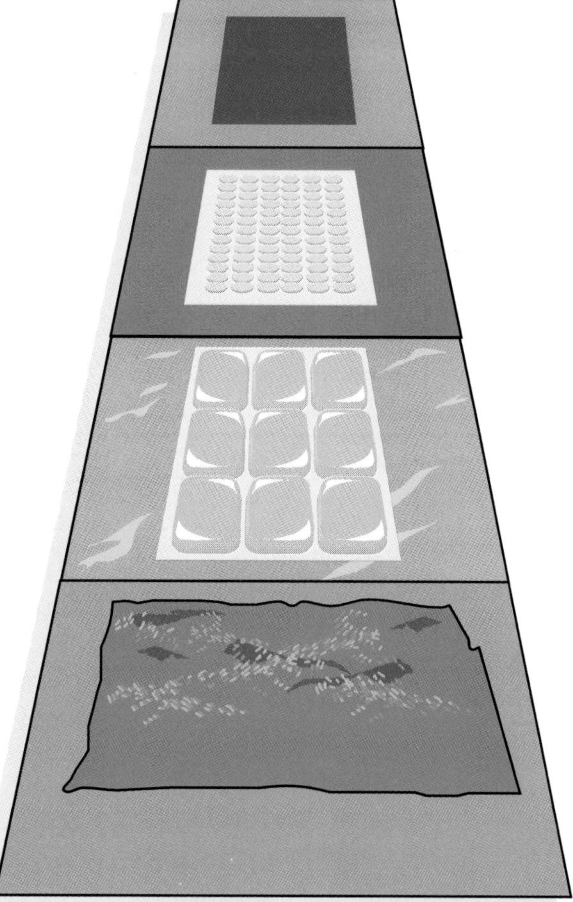

A Trip Down Texture Trail

Take youngsters on a trip down texture lane with this creative idea. To make a texture trail, laminate ten 12" x 18" sheets of construction paper. Tape the sheets together end-to-end so that when spread on the floor, a 12" x 180" trail is created. On each sheet of paper, adhere a section of a uniquely textured material such as bubble wrap, sandpaper, fake fur, vinyl, or felt. Attempt to include on the trail materials with as great a variety of color and density as possible.

Encourage children to explore the texture trail by feeling each texture with their hands, crawling along the trail, or walking barefoot down the trail. As a language extension, ask children to help you describe the attributes of each section of the trail. To store the trail, simply fold it accordion-style. Happy trails to you!

Linda Becker—Pre-K
Parents Are Important in Rochester
Rochester, MN

Appealing to the Senses

Children can benefit from a variety of multisensory experiences. Make a multisensory pack by pouring three cups of a substance (selected from the suggestions that follow) into a gallon-size, resealable plastic bag. Squeeze the air out of the bag as much as possible before sealing the bag shut. To use this pack, have a child flatten it on a tabletop and "write" or draw on it with a finger.

Suggested items for filling a pack:

- September—green shampoo to which 1/2 cup of apple seeds has been added
- October—white milk bath tinted with orange food coloring
- November—commercially prepared chocolate pudding
- December—clear cooking oil with red and green glitter
- January—white glue
- February—clear dishwashing detergent with heart-shaped foil confetti
- March—green dishwashing detergent
- April—deep yellow or golden shampoo
- May—white milk bath tinted with red food coloring

Mary Carlin—Special Education
Live Oak Elementary
Baton Rouge, LA

Scented Ink Pads

If you have a few drops of scented oil to spare, here's a great tip that makes "scents." Simply apply a few drops of an oil fragrance onto a colored ink pad. Then invite youngsters to make their own ink-stamp creations. What a wonderful blend of designs and scents!

Sue Lewis Lein—Four-Year-Old K
St. Pius X School
Wauwatosa, WI

Wiggle Worm Words

Squeeze in a little language practice with this sensory snack idea. Give each child a napkin, Gummy Worm candies, and pretzel sticks. Invite him to create letters and words with the foods before eating. The worms bend into curvy letters *(O, S, C)* and the pretzels make straight letters *(A, H, T)*. What kinds of words will your students cook up?

Kelly Larson—Gr. K
St. Joseph Grade School
Shawnee, KS

Let's Make Some Noise

Follow up a reading of a noisy story, such as Rosemary Wells's *Noisy Nora* with this fun song. Instruct each youngster to look around the room for something that makes noise or for some way to create a noise. Then have each child, in turn, make his noise during one round of the verse below.

(sung to the tune of "Old MacDonald")

[Teacher's name] had a class.
Bing! Bang! Bing! Bang! Boom!
And in her class there was a noise.
Bing! Bang! Bing! Bang! Boom!
With a *(child makes noise)* here and a *(child makes noise)* there.
Here a *(child makes noise),* there a *(child makes noise),*
Everywhere a *(child makes a noise).*
[Teacher's name] had a class.
Bing! Bang! Bing! Bang! Boom!

Patricia Moeser
Madison, WI

Sing a Song of Senses

Add a little song to your five-senses study with this catchy tune.

(sung to the tune of "The Farmer in the Dell")

We use our tongues to taste.
We use our tongues to taste.
We taste the flavors in our food.
We use our tongues to taste.

We use our ears to hear.
We use our ears to hear.
We hear noises loud and soft.
We use our ears to hear.

We use our eyes to see.
We use our eyes to see.
We see colors all around.
We use our eyes to see.

We use our noses to smell.
We use our noses to smell.
We smell flowers and perfume.
We use our noses to smell.

We use our hands to touch.
We use our hands to touch.
We touch things both smooth and rough.
We use our hands to touch.

Dianne Gleason—Gr. K
Preston Hollow Elementary
Dallas, TX

Five-Senses Book

Watch your youngsters' sense of excitement soar when making this five-senses book. To make a book, staple five sheets of white construction paper between two pieces of tagboard. Label each of the five pages with one of the five senses. Glue a small amount of the following items on the appropriate pages: foil (sight), sandpaper (touch and hearing), cotton ball (touch), smelly sticker (smell), stick of sugarless gum (taste). To extend this activity, label a table in your room as the sensory table and place a variety of things for each of the five senses on it. Have your students try to determine which objects are related to one or more of the senses. Sounds "sense-able"!

Linda Schwitzke—Preschool
Headstart Preschool
Longview, WA

"Sense-sational" Starfish

This craft uses a fabulous textured paint with lots of sensory appeal! To prepare, mix several different colors of puff paint. For each color, combine two tablespoons of washable tempera paint and one-third cup of white glue. Fold in two cups of nonmentholated shaving cream until the color is well blended. (For best results, use the paint soon after mixing it.)

To make one starfish, fingerpaint a star-shaped tagboard cutout with several colors of the puff paint. Sprinkle glitter over the wet paint; then set the starfish aside to dry overnight. Youngsters will enjoy smelling, touching, and seeing this interesting paint—even when it's dry!

Beverly Folena—Pre-K
Creative Kids Preschool
Placerville, CA

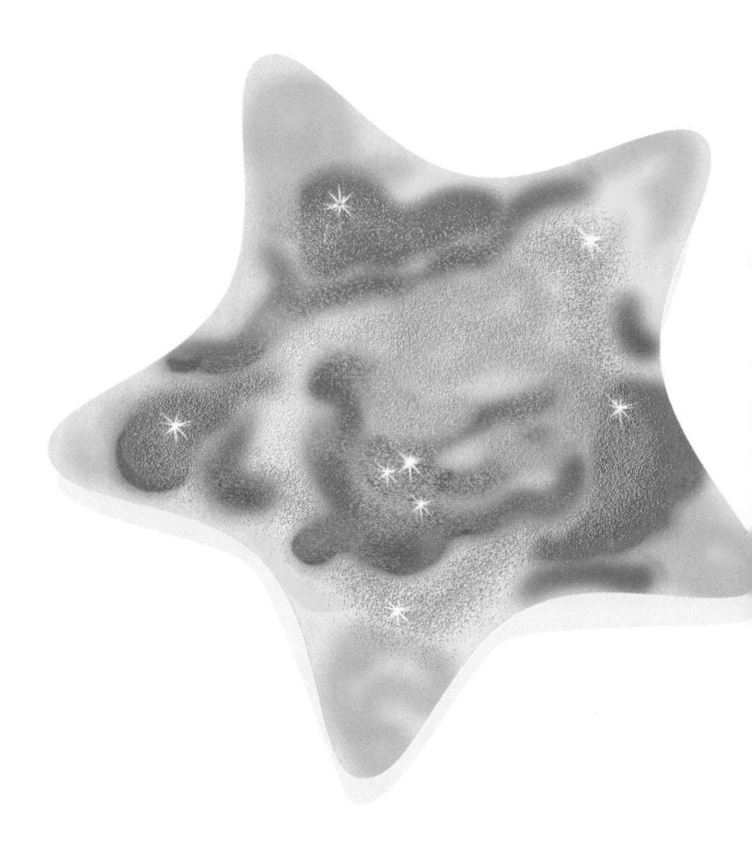

Fruity Putty

Invite youngsters to sculpt fruit likenesses using different colors of this fruity-smelling dough.

0.3-ounce package of sugar-free, fruit-flavored gelatin
2 cups flour
1 cup salt
4 tablespoons cream of tartar
2 cups boiling water
2 tablespoons cooking oil

Mix the dry ingredients in a pan. Add the boiling water and cooking oil. Stir over medium-high heat until the mixture forms a ball. Place the ball on waxed paper to cool. Store in an airtight container. Cut the fruit picture from the gelatin box and attach it to the lid of the container to label it.

Cynthia Zsittnik—Preschool
Surrey Child Care Center
Hagerstown, MD

Sensory Counting Box

Review numbers during circle time with this super sensory idea. Create a counting box by filling a small plastic tub with a sensory material, such as rice, sand, or dried beans. Each day, bury a specific number of thematic mini erasers in the tub. Write the corresponding numeral and draw a matching set of dots on a small dry-erase board. Place the board near the tub. Ask a volunteer to identify the numeral on the board; then have her find the corresponding number of erasers. After completing the activity at circle time, hide the erasers again and make the box and board available at your sensory center during free play.

Tami Bertini—Early Childhood Special Education
Bondurant-Farrar Community Schools
Bondurant, IA

Sniff, Sniff

Surprise youngsters with scented paper for increased interest in journal writing. Before school starts one morning, use a cotton ball to dab a colorless extract, such as peppermint or vanilla, onto a page in each child's journal. You're sure to get some sweet writing in return!

adapted from an idea by John M. Barrera
Las Americas Early Childhood Development Center
Houston, TX

Textures and Scents

Heighten interest in certain classroom activities by adding textures and scents to create multisensory experiences. For example, adding salt to fingerpaint gives it an interesting new texture. If you have a water-play area, add mint, cinnamon, or other pleasant scents to the water. This encourages children to be aware of and use all of their available senses.

Kimberly L. Barnes—Preschool Special Needs
Delphi Community Schools
Delphi, IN

Feeling Is Believing

Smooth out the rough spots of number recognition with this sensory sensation. Using cardboard patterns, trace and cut out each of the numbers 0 through 9 from both sandpaper and poster board. Glue each sandpaper cutout atop its matching poster board counterpart. Place the cutouts inside an old top hat or "magic bag." Then blindfold a volunteer from the audience and ask him to draw a number. Wave your "magic wand" above him as you say, "Alakazam!" Then have him amaze the audience by feeling the cutout and revealing its identity.

Sweet Dreams

At naptime help your little ones relax into a state of sweet dreams with this extra bit of "in-scent-ive." Fill a spray bottle with water; then add a few drops of vanilla extract. Label the outside of the bottle "Sweet Dreams." During naptime, spray a mist of the solution over the heads of your little ones.

Elizabeth A. Cooper
Meadowbrook Elementary School
Fort Worth, TX

Jingle Bells! Jingle Bells!

Jingle all the way with these easy-to-make instruments. To make one, cut a strip of plastic canvas one inch wide and about eight inches long. Use yarn to sew three jingle bells onto the strip. Bring both ends of the strip together to form a circle; then sew the ends together with yarn. If desired, yarn can also be sewn around the edges of the band for a decorative border.

Julia Elsen
Thatcher, AR

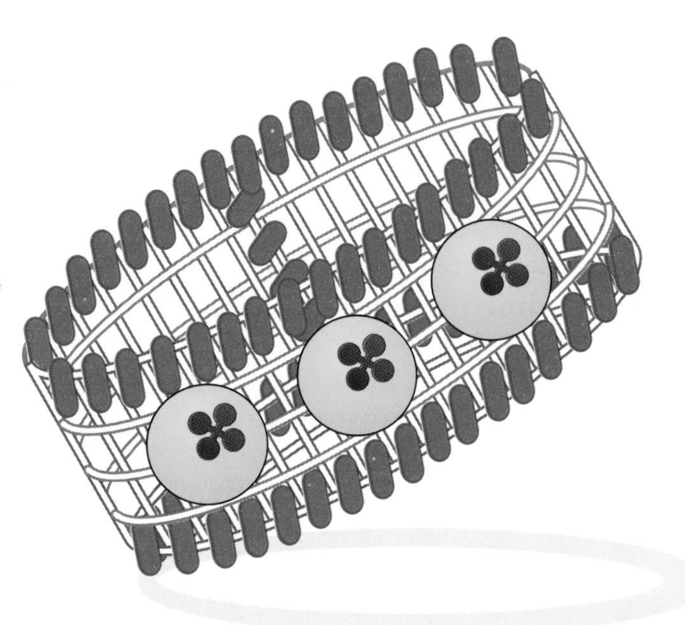

Reproducible Activities...

from Teacher's Helper® magazine

How to Use Page 33

Encourage children to touch their five sense organs as you say their names: eyes, nose, ears, mouth/tongue, and hands/skin. Ask children to find these sense organs on the picture of the boy on the worksheet. Children should then paste them in the correct boxes as you read the oral instructions.

Oral Instructions

1. We use different parts of our body to see, hear, smell, taste, and touch. Listen and help me decide where to paste the words you have cut out.
2. We use our ears to...*(wait for response)*. That's right, *hear.* Paste the word *hear* above the boy's ear.
3. We use our eyes to...*(wait for response)*. That's right, *see.* Paste the word *see* next to the boy's eye.
4. We use our nose to...*(wait for response)*. That's right, *smell.* Paste the word *smell* next to the boy's nose.
5. We use our mouth (and tongue) to...*(wait for response)*. That's right, *taste.* Paste the word *taste* next to the boy's mouth.
6. We use our hands (and skin) to...*(wait for response)*. That's right, *touch.* Paste the word *touch* next to the boy's hand.

Background for the Teacher

Our Senses

The five senses are quite familiar to the child by the time he reaches kindergarten. Children should be able to identify the sense organs as the eyes, ears, nose, mouth (or tongue), and skin (or hands). The sense organs are the "information gatherers" which send sensory information via nerves to the brain.

Some basic facts your children should be able to understand are:

We need light in order to see. The pupil in the eye adjusts to the amount of light in a room to allow as much light as possible to reach the retina in the eye. That is why the pupil dilates in darkness—it is attempting to allow as much light as possible to get to the retina.

Sounds are really air vibrations which reach the ear, causing vibrations in the ear as well. When one has an ear infection, sounds are muffled because the air vibrations cannot move as freely through the liquid which often collects in an infected ear.

The senses of smell and taste must often work together. In order to properly taste something, it is necessary to also be able to smell it. That is why, when one has a cold, foods often taste blander.

The sense of touch includes the senses of pressure, pain, and temperature. We usually associate the sense of touch with the fingers because they are the most sensitive due to the high concentration of nerve endings in the fingers. This should not overshadow the fact that the entire body, via the skin, is sensitive to and can send information to the brain through the sense of touch.

Name ____

Our Five Senses

Cut and glue.

We use different parts of our bodies to

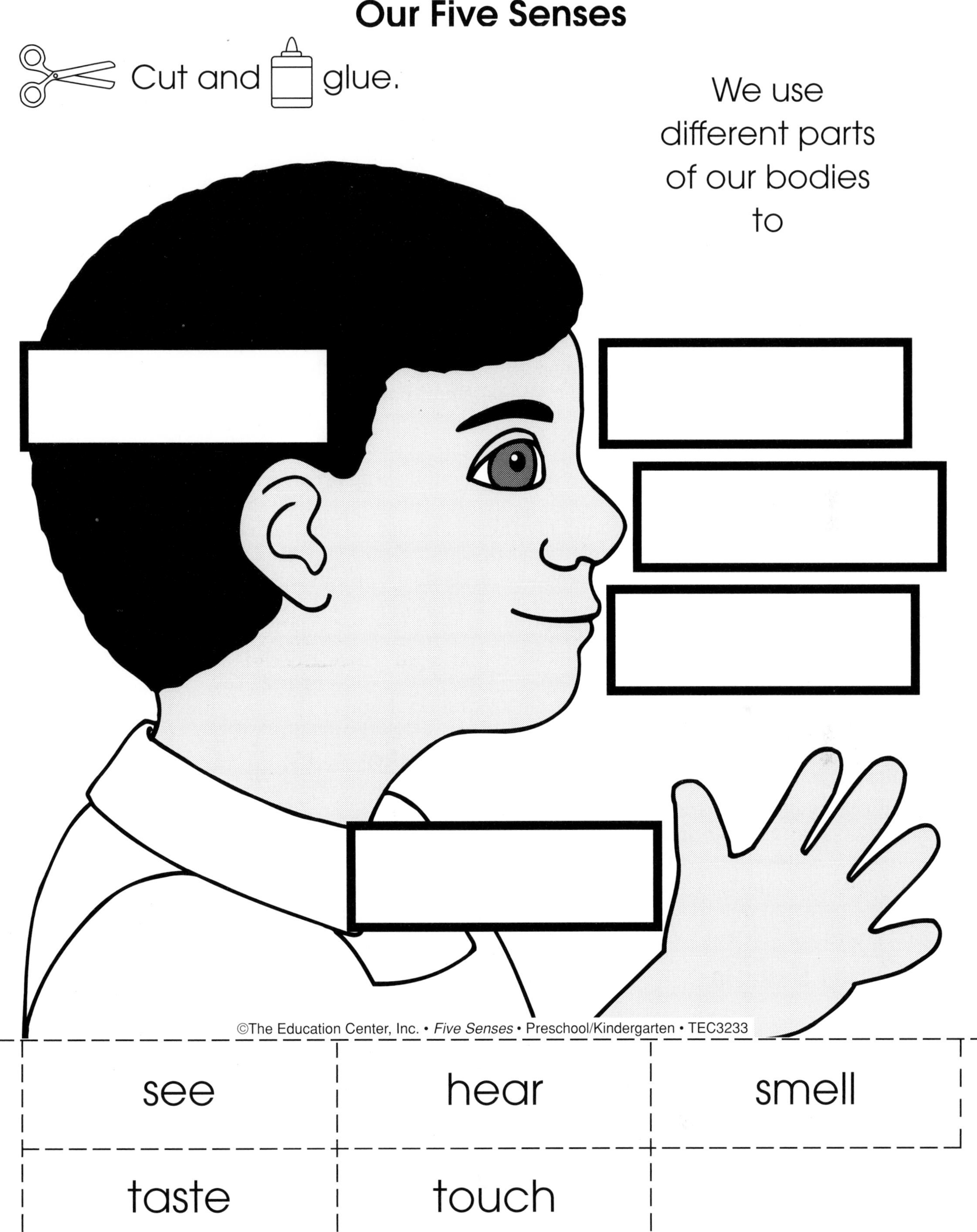

see	hear	smell
taste	touch	

How to Use Page 35

Challenge youngsters to use their sense of hearing to complete this activity. Read the following oral instructions.

Oral Instructions

Find the thing that makes a
...splashing sound. (water) Color the water blue.
...chop-chop sound. (knife) Draw a red circle around the knife.
...swish-swish sound. (broom) Color the broom yellow.
...whirring sound. (blender) Color the blender purple.
...tick, tick, ding! sound. (timer) Draw a green circle around the timer.
...crash, bang sound. (pots/pans) Color the pots and pans orange.

Variation

Record each sound for about 30 seconds in the following order: water running, knife chopping, broom sweeping, blender running, timer ticking and ringing, pots and pans banging. Play the recordings as you introduce each item on the worksheet. Pause after each sound as children find the matching item. Instruct children to color or circle items as you read the instructions.

1. *(Play the sound of water running.)* What makes that sound? Yes, water running. Color the water blue.
2. *(Play the sound of the knife chopping.)* What makes that sound? Yes, the knife chopping. Draw a red circle around the knife.
3. *(Play the sound of a broom sweeping.)* What makes that sound? Yes, the broom sweeping the floor. Color the broom yellow.
4. *(Play the sound of the blender running.)* What makes that sound? Yes, the blender. Color the blender purple.
5. *(Play the sound of the timer.)* What makes that sound? Yes, the timer. Draw a green circle around the timer.
6. *(Play the sound of the pots and pans.)* What makes that sound? Yes, the pots and pans. Color the pots and pans orange.

Finished Sample

Name ____________________

Noisy Kitchen Chorus

You **HEAR** sounds with your **EARS.**
Listen and do.

How to Use Page 37

Bring in food items shown on the worksheet for the children to taste. Discuss which foods are *sweet, sour,* and *salty.* Write the three words on the chalkboard. Help children identify the words sweet, sour, and salty on the worksheet. Then have each child complete his worksheet. (The worksheet can be presented without the tasting activity.)

Extension Activities

— Blindfold children and encourage them to guess what they are tasting, first stating if the food is sweet, sour, or salty.

— Have the children hold their noses during a tasting party. Why did the food not taste distinct? Emphasize that the senses of smell and taste often work together.

Name ______________________________

Tasty Tidbits

You **TASTE** with your **MOUTH** and **TONGUE.**

 Cut and  glue.

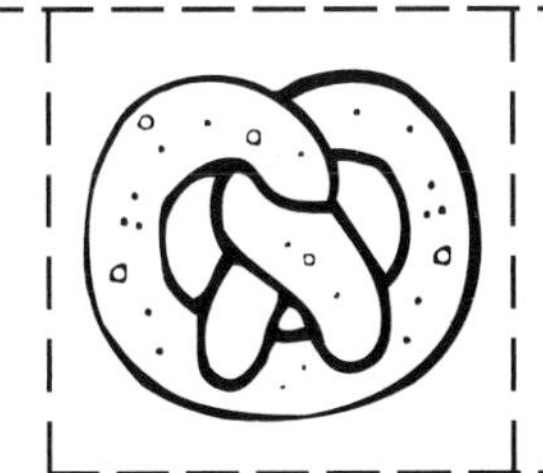    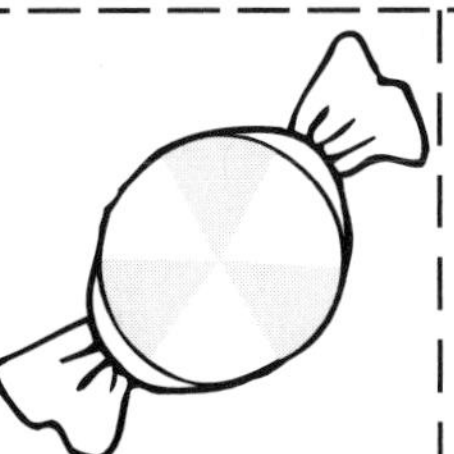 

How to Use Page 39

Invite students to recall their sense of smell to complete this activity. Read the following oral instructions.

Oral Instructions

1. The girl is using her nose to tell her what foods are on the table.
2. What food smells like lemons? Lemonade. Color the lemonade yellow.
3. What food smells like apples? Apple pie. Draw a red square around the pie.
4. What food smells like cinnamon? Cinnamon rolls. Draw a purple triangle on the rolls.
5. What food smells like chocolate? Chocolate cake. Color the cake brown.
6. What food smells burned? Toast. Color the toast black.
7. What food smells strong and sharp? Onion. Draw a green circle around the onion.

Extension Activity

Bring in food samples for your children to smell. Put small portions of the following in individual margarine tubs with small holes punched in the lids:

- burned toast
- ground cinnamon
- lemon wedge
- apple slice
- onion slice
- chocolate chips

Allow the children to smell foods while blindfolded, and encourage them to guess what they smell.

Name ______________________________

What Do I Smell?

You **SMELL** with your **NOSE.**
Listen and do.

How to Use Page 41

Present the following kitchen items for children to describe as rough, soft, or hard:

scrub brush and grater (rough)
dish towel and pot holder (soft)
cup and spoon (hard)

Complete the worksheet, helping children to identify the words *rough, soft,* and *hard.*

Extension Activities

— Ask children to close their eyes and touch the kitchen items. Encourage them to guess what they are touching, first stating whether the item is rough, soft, or hard. Include additional kitchen items to expand the activity.

— Collect an assortment of small items which are distinct in their shape (marble, small counting cube, small doll's spoon, small car, etc.). Push the items into balloons. Inflate the balloons very slightly and tie the ends. Place in a box and encourage the children to feel the item through the balloon and guess what is inside. This same idea can be done with larger items, using old socks instead of balloons.

How to Use Page 43

Have students recall all five senses as they complete this page. Read the following oral instructions.

Oral Instructions

1. Find the box with the eyes in it. The box says: "I use my eyes to…(*see*)." Trace the word *see.* In the box, draw a picture of something you see that is round.
2. Find the box with the nose in it. The box says: "I use my nose to…(*smell*)." Trace the word *smell.* Draw a picture of something that smells good.
3. Find the box with the ears in it. The box says: "I use my ears to…(*hear*)." Trace the word *hear.* Draw a picture of something you hear that is loud.
4. Find the box with the mouth and tongue in it. The box says: "I use my mouth and tongue to…(*taste*)." Trace the word *taste.* Draw a picture of something that tastes sweet.
5. Find the box with the hands in it. The box says: "I use my hands to…(*touch*)." Trace the word *touch.* Draw a picture of something that is soft.

Name____

Hands-On Cooking

You **TOUCH** with your **HANDS.**

Cut and glue.

Name______________________

Cookie Cutter Shape-Up

You **SEE** shapes and colors with your **EYES.**

Draw lines to match.

Color each cookie a different color.

How many different colors do you see? ________

Name ____________________

Using Your Senses

Listen and do.

How do you use your five senses?

 Trace. Color.

I use my to see.

I use my to smell.

I use my to hear.

I use my to taste.

I use my to touch.

Background for the Teacher

People and animals use their senses to find out about the world around them. Our five main senses are hearing, sight, smell, taste, and touch. These senses collect information from outside the body, and then nerves or receptors take the message to the brain. Our brain interprets each message, making us aware of the sound, sight, smell, taste, or touch that we are experiencing.

How to Use Page 45

1. Color and cut out the patterns at the bottom of the page.
2. Match each pattern piece to the cat and glue in place.
3. Look at each sentence below the cat and decide which word (hear, see, smell, taste, or touch) will correctly finish it.
4. Write the action word to complete each sentence.

Finished Sample

Name ____

"Purr-fect" Sense

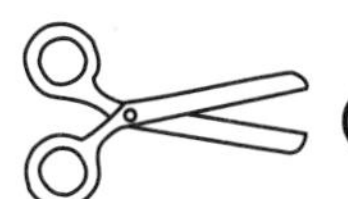 Cut.  Glue. Write.

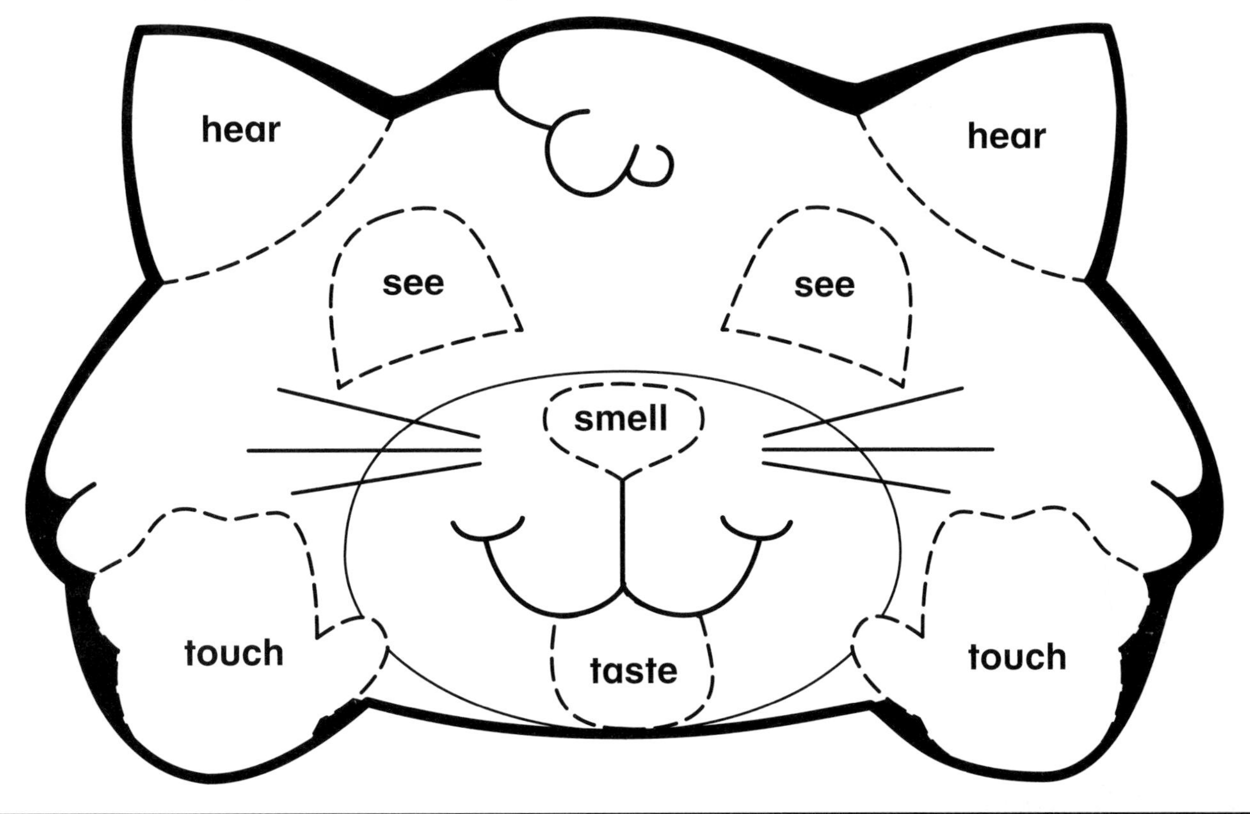

Eyes ____________. Ears ____________. Noses ____________.

Tongues ____________. Fingers ____________.

Name ______________________________

Sounds Sweet!

We hear with our **ears.**
We taste with our **tongues.**

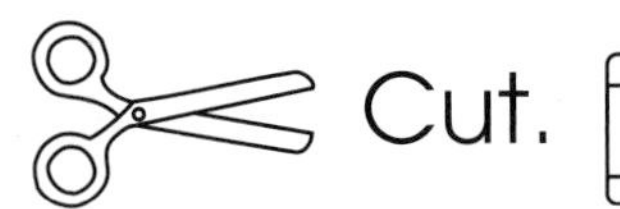 Cut.  Glue.

hear	taste

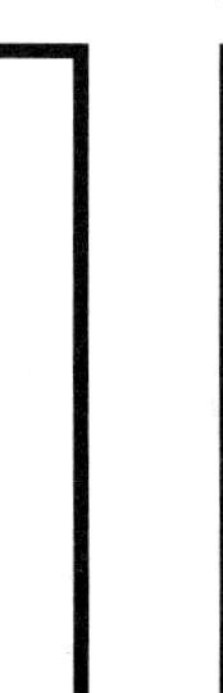

Draw.

I like to hear…

I like to taste…

Name____

Hands Down!

We touch with our **hands.**

We smell with our **noses.**

 Cut.  Glue.

touch	smell

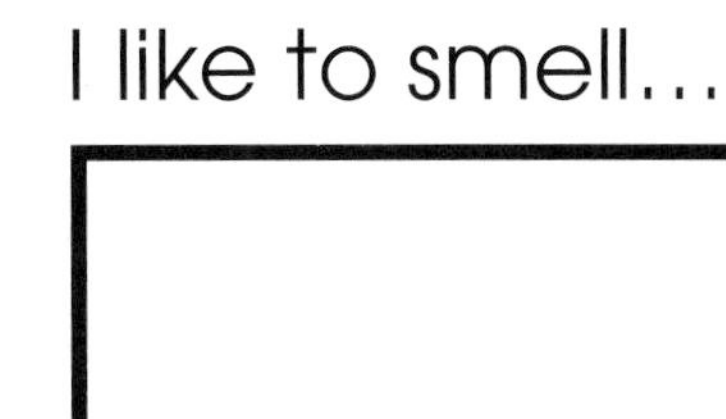

Draw.

I like to touch...

I like to smell...

Name ____

Seeing Is Believing

We see with our **eyes.**
Draw what you see **now.**

Sometimes we use our senses together.

Color the senses you could use for each one.

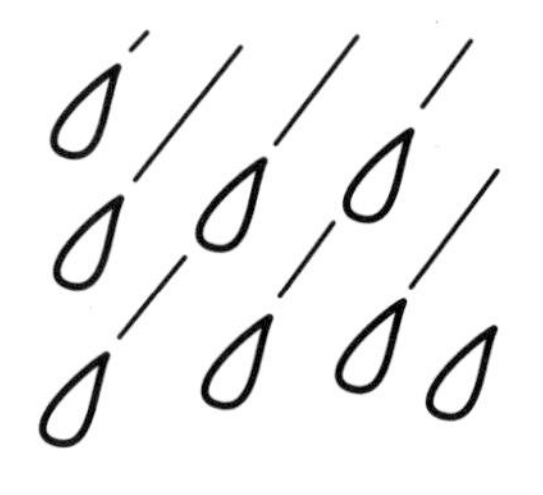 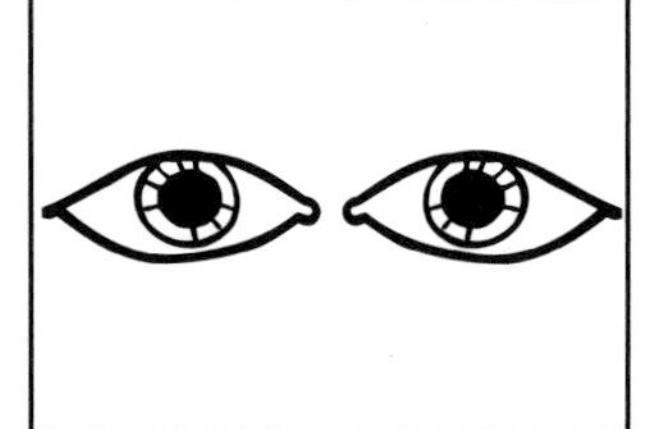  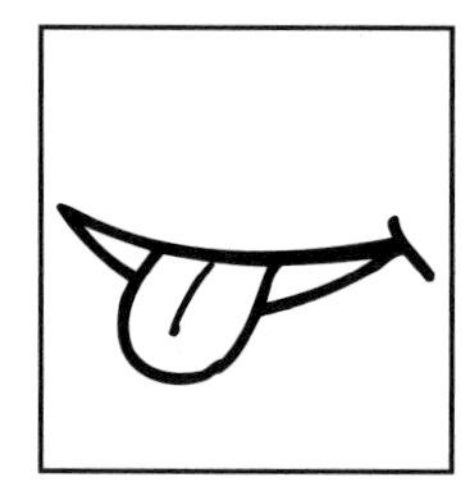 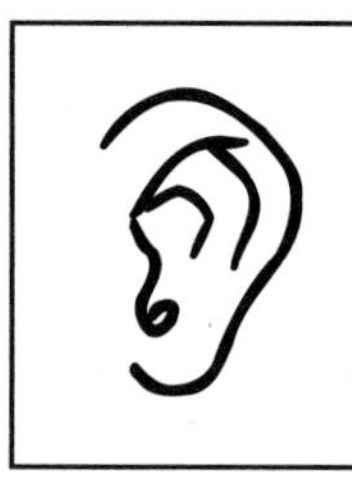 

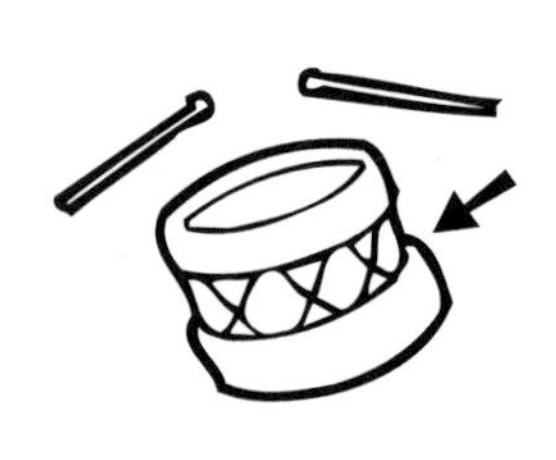   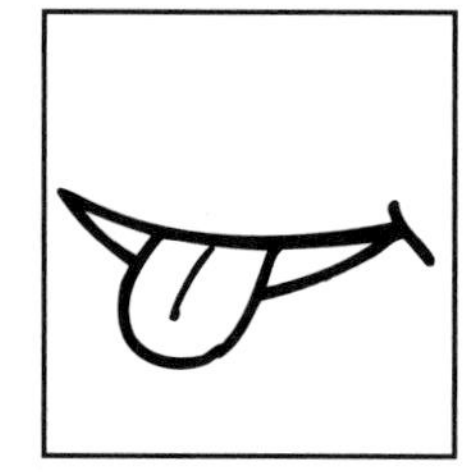 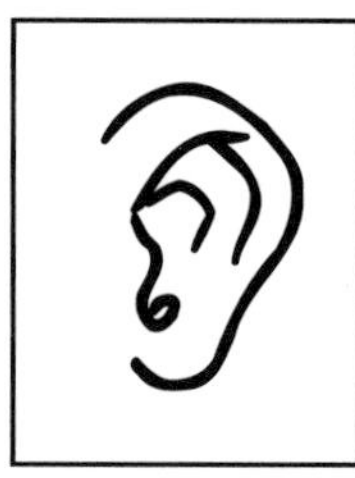 

   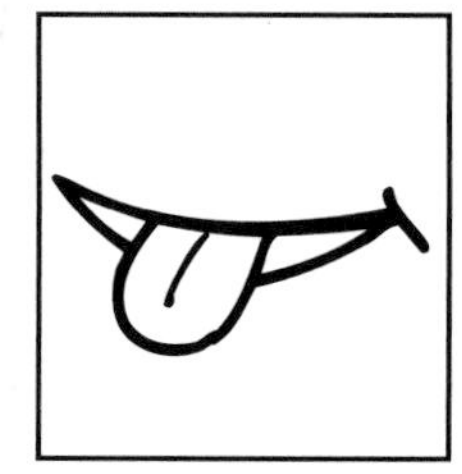  

  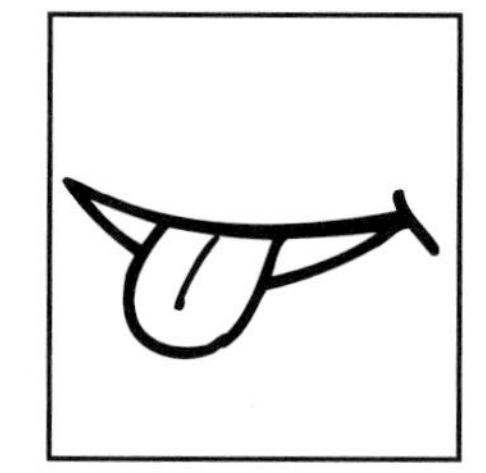  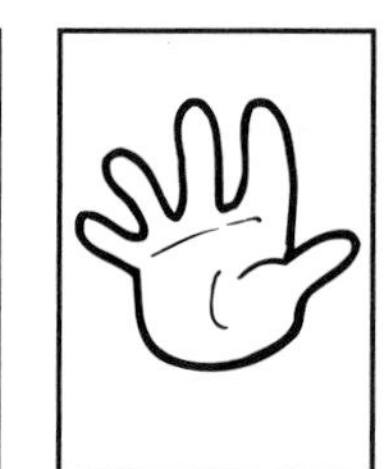